This journal belongs to

Belle City Gifts
Racine, Wisconsin, USA

Belle City Gifts is an imprint of BroadStreet Publishing Group LLC.
Broadstreetpublishing.com

Bible Promises for Mothers

© 2015 by BroadStreet Publishing

ISBN 978-1-4245-5455-3

Compiled by Michelle Winger | www.literallyprecise.com
Design by Chris Garborg | www.garborgdesign.com

Printed in China.

15 16 17 18 19 20 21   7 6 5 4 3 2 1

BIBLE PROMISES FOR
Mothers
JOURNAL

Contents

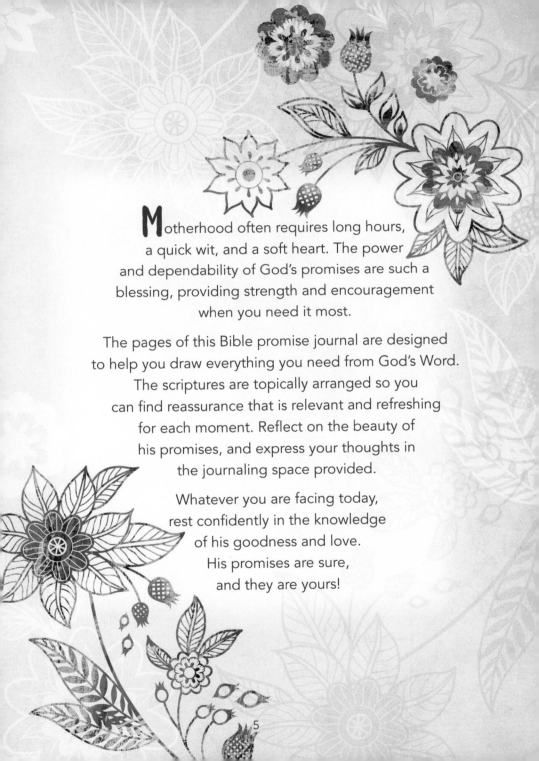

Motherhood often requires long hours, a quick wit, and a soft heart. The power and dependability of God's promises are such a blessing, providing strength and encouragement when you need it most.

The pages of this Bible promise journal are designed to help you draw everything you need from God's Word. The scriptures are topically arranged so you can find reassurance that is relevant and refreshing for each moment. Reflect on the beauty of his promises, and express your thoughts in the journaling space provided.

Whatever you are facing today, rest confidently in the knowledge of his goodness and love. His promises are sure, and they are yours!

Acceptance

Before he made the world, God chose us to be his very own through what Christ would do for us; he decided then to make us holy in his eyes, without a single fault— we who stand before him covered with his love.

EPHESIANS 1:4 TLB

"Don't be afraid, because I have saved you.
I have called you by name, and you are mine.
When you pass through the waters, I will be with you.
When you cross rivers, you will not drown.
When you walk through fire, you will not be burned,
nor will the flames hurt you.
Because you are precious to me,
because I give you honor and love you,
I will give other people in your place;
I will give other nations to save your life."

ISAIAH 43:1-2, 4 NCV

If God is for us, who can be against us?

ROMANS 8:31 ESV

"Here I am! I stand at the door and knock. If anyone hears my voice and opens the door, I will come in and eat with that person, and they with me."

REVELATION 3:20 NIV

Adoption

You did not receive a spirit of slavery to fall back into fear, but you have received a spirit of adoption. When we cry, "Abba! Father!" it is that very Spirit bearing witness with our spirit that we are children of God.

ROMANS 8:15–16 NRSV

A father of the fatherless and a judge for the widows,
Is God in His holy habitation.
God makes a home for the lonely;
He leads out the prisoners into prosperity.

PSALM 68:5-6 NASB

As many as received Him, to them He gave the right to become children of God, even to those who believe in His name.

JOHN 1:12 NASB

When the right time came, God sent his Son, born of a woman, subject to the law. God sent him to buy freedom for us who were slaves to the law, so that he could adopt us as his very own children.

GALATIANS 4:4-5 NLT

"The Father gives me the people who are mine. Every one of them will come to me, and I will always accept them."

JOHN 6:37 NCV

Affection

My God is changeless in his love for me,
and he will come and help me.

PSALM 59:10 TLB

I am my beloved's,
And his desire is toward me.

SONG OF SOLOMON 7:10 NKJV

Carry each other's burdens, and in this way you will
fulfill the law of Christ.... As we have opportunity,
llet us do good to all people.

GALATIANS 6:2, 10 NIV

You make known to me the path of life;
you will fill me with joy in your presence,
with eternal pleasures at your right hand.

PSALM 16:11 NIV

"The LORD your God is living among you.
He is a mighty savior.
He will take delight in you with gladness.
With his love, he will calm all your fears.
He will rejoice over you with joyful songs."

ZEPHANIAH 3:17 NLT

"Arise, my love, my beautiful one,
and come away,
for behold, the winter is past;
the rain is over and gone.
The flowers appear on the earth,
the time of singing has come."

SONG OF SOLOMON 2:10-12 ESV

Anger

Be not quick in your spirit to become angry,
for anger lodges in the heart of fools.

ECCLESIASTES 7:9 ESV

Everyone should be quick to listen, slow to speak and slow to
become angry, because human anger does not produce the
righteousness that God desires.

JAMES 1:19–20 NIV

Sensible people control their temper;
they earn respect by overlooking wrongs.

PROVERBS 19:11 NLT

A fool vents all his feelings,
But a wise man holds them back.

PROVERBS 29:11 NKJV

Whatever is true, whatever is noble, whatever is right,
whatever is pure, whatever is lovely, whatever is admirable—
if anything is excellent or praiseworthy—
think about such things.

PHILIPPIANS 4:8 NIV

Whoever is slow to anger has great understanding.

PROVERBS 14:29 ESV

Do not be overcome by evil, but overcome evil with good.

ROMANS 12:21 NRSV

"In your anger do not sin": Do not let the sun go down while
you are still angry, and do not give the devil a foothold.

EPHESIANS 4:26–27 NIV

Anxiety

Do not be anxious about anything, but in every situation,
by prayer and petition, with thanksgiving,
present your requests to God.

PHILIPPIANS 4:6 NIV

Cast all your anxiety on him because he cares for you.

1 PETER 5:7 NIV

If you make the LORD your refuge,
if you make the Most High your shelter,
no evil will conquer you;
no plague will come near your home.
For he will order his angels
to protect you wherever you go.

PSALM 91:9–11 NLT

"I have said these things to you, that in me you may have
peace. In the world you will have tribulation. But take heart;
I have overcome the world."

JOHN 16:33 ESV

In my trouble I cried to the LORD,
And He answered me.

PSALM 120:1 NASB

"Let not your heart be troubled. You are trusting God,
now trust in me."

JOHN 14:1 TLB

"Be strong, and do not fear,
for your God...is coming to save you."

ISAIAH 35:4 NLT

Authenticity

"It's not *where* we worship that counts, but *how* we worship—is our worship spiritual and real? Do we have the Holy Spirit's help? For God is Spirit, and we must have his help to worship as we should. The Father wants this kind of worship from us."

JOHN 4:23–24 TLB

"Whoever makes himself great will be made humble. Whoever makes himself humble will be made great."

MATTHEW 23:12 NCV

I plead with you to give your bodies to God. Let them be a living sacrifice, holy—the kind he can accept. When you think of what he has done for you, is this too much to ask? Don't copy the behavior and customs of this world, but be a new and different person with a fresh newness in all you do and think. Then you will learn from your own experience how his ways will really satisfy you.

ROMANS 12:1–2 TLB

He gives more grace. Therefore He says:
"God resists the proud,
But gives grace to the humble."

JAMES 4:6 NKJV

Beauty

I will praise You,
for I am fearfully and wonderfully made;
Marvelous are Your works,
And that my soul knows very well.

PSALM 139:14 NKJV

Don't be concerned about the outward beauty of fancy hairstyles, expensive jewelry, or beautiful clothes. You should clothe yourselves instead with the beauty that comes from within, the unfading beauty of a gentle and quiet spirit, which is so precious to God.

1 PETER 3:3–4 NLT

"You cannot add any time to your life by worrying about it. And why do you worry about clothes? Look at how the lilies in the field grow. They don't work or make clothes for themselves. But I tell you that even Solomon with his riches was not dressed as beautifully as one of these flowers. God clothes the grass in the field, which is alive today but tomorrow is thrown into the fire. So you can be even more sure that God will clothe you. Don't have so little faith!"

MATTHEW 6:27–29 NCV

The LORD doesn't see things the way you see them.
People judge by outward appearance,
but the LORD looks at the heart.

1 SAMUEL 16:7 NLT

Blessings

From his abundance we have all received one gracious blessing after another.

JOHN 1:16 NLT

The LORD bless you, and keep you;
The LORD make His face shine on you,
And be gracious to you;
The LORD lift up His countenance on you,
And give you peace.

NUMBERS 6:24–26 NASB

You prepare a feast for me
in the presence of my enemies.
You honor me by anointing my head with oil.
My cup overflows with blessings.

PSALM 23:5 NLT

Blessed be the God and Father of our Lord Jesus Christ, who has blessed us in Christ with every spiritual blessing in the heavenly places, even as he chose us in him before the foundation of the world.

EPHESIANS 1:3–4 ESV

Taste and see that the LORD is good;
blessed is the one who takes refuge in him!

PSALM 34:8 NIV

Happy are those who are strong in the Lord, who want above all else to follow your steps. When they walk through the Valley of Weeping, it will become a place of springs where pools of blessing and refreshment collect after rains!

PSALM 84:5–6 TLB

Caring

"I was hungry and you gave me something to eat, I was thirsty and you gave me something to drink, I was a stranger and you invited me in, I needed clothes and you clothed me, I was sick and you looked after me, I was in prison and you came to visit me.... Whatever you did for one of the least of these brothers and sisters of mine, you did for me."

MATTHEW 25:35–36, 40 NIV

Do not merely look out for your own personal interests, but also for the interests of others.

PHILIPPIANS 2:4 NASB

Bear one another's burdens, and so fulfill the law of Christ.

GALATIANS 6:2 ESV

If anyone has material possessions and sees a brother or sister in need but has no pity on them, how can the love of God be in that person? Dear children, let us not love with words or speech but with actions and in truth.

1 JOHN 3:17–18 NIV

Pure and genuine religion in the sight of God the Father means caring for orphans and widows in their distress.

JAMES 1:27 NLT

Change

There is a time for everything,
and everything on earth has its special season.

ECCLESIASTES 3:1 NCV

"Unless you change and become like little children, you will never enter the kingdom of heaven."

MATTHEW 18:3 NIV

We shall not all sleep, but we shall all be changed.

1 CORINTHIANS 15:51 NKJV

He will take our weak mortal bodies and change them into glorious bodies like his own, using the same power with which he will bring everything under his control.

PHILIPPIANS 3:21 NLT

Our faces, then, are not covered. We all show the Lord's glory, and we are being changed to be like him. This change in us brings ever greater glory, which comes from the Lord, who is the Spirit.

2 CORINTHIANS 3:18 NCV

Jesus Christ is the same yesterday and today and forever.

HEBREWS 13:8 NASB

Every good gift and every perfect gift is from above, coming down from the Father of lights with whom there is no variation or shadow due to change.

JAMES 1:17 ESV

Children

Direct your children onto the right path,
and when they are older, they will not leave it.

PROVERBS 22:6 NLT

These words which I command you today shall be in your
heart. You shall teach them diligently to your children, and
shall talk of them when you sit in your house, when you walk
by the way, when you lie down, and when you rise up.

DEUTERONOMY 6:6–7 NKJV

"Let the little children come to Me,
and do not forbid them;
for of such is the kingdom of heaven."

MATTHEW 19:14 NKJV

Those who spare the rod hate their children,
but those who love them are diligent to discipline them.

PROVERBS 13:24 NRSV

"Any of you who welcomes a little child like this because you
are mine, is welcoming me.... Don't look down upon a single
one of these little children. For I tell you that in heaven their
angels have constant access to my Father."

MATTHEW 18:5, 10 TLB

Children are a gift from the LORD; they are a reward from him.

PSALM 127:3 NLT

I have no greater joy than to hear that my children are
walking in the truth.

3 JOHN 1:4 NIV

Companionship

God makes a home for the lonely;
He leads out the prisoners into prosperity.

PSALM 68:6 NASB

Those who know your name trust in you,
for you, O LORD, do not abandon
those who search for you.

PSALM 9:10 NLT

"I will bring the blind by a way they did not know;
I will lead them in paths they have not known.
I will make darkness light before them,
And crooked places straight.
These things will I do for them,
And not forsake them."

ISAIAH 42:16 NKJV

"The LORD will not abandon His people on account of His great name, because the LORD has been pleased to make you a people for Himself."

1 SAMUEL 12:22 NASB

"I will not abandon you as orphans—I will come to you."

JOHN 14:18 NLT

"The LORD himself goes before you and will be with you; he will never leave you nor forsake you."

DEUTERONOMY 31:8 NIV

Compassion

The LORD longs to be gracious to you;
therefore he will rise up to show you compassion.
For the LORD is a God of justice.
Blessed are all who wait for him!

ISAIAH 30:18 NIV

You, O Lord, are a God full of compassion, and gracious,
Longsuffering and abundant in mercy and truth.

PSALM 86:15 NKJV

Where is another God like you, who pardons the sins
of the survivors among his people? You cannot
stay angry with your people, for you love to be merciful.
Once again you will have compassion on us. You will tread
our sins beneath your feet; you will throw them into
the depths of the ocean! You will bless us as you
promised Jacob long ago. You will set your love upon us,
as you promised our father Abraham!

MICAH 7:18–20 TLB

Be gracious to me, O God,
according to Your lovingkindness;
According to the greatness of Your compassion
blot out my transgressions.

PSALM 51:1 NASB

Praise be to the God and Father of our Lord Jesus Christ,
the Father of compassion and the God of all comfort.

2 CORINTHIANS 1:3 NIV

Confidence

Be my rock of refuge,
to which I can always go;
give the command to save me,
for you are my rock and my fortress....
You have been my hope, Sovereign LORD,
my confidence since my youth.

PSALM 71:3, 5 NIV

I can do everything through Christ, who gives me strength.

PHILIPPIANS 4:13 NLT

The LORD will be your confidence,
And will keep your foot from being caught.

PROVERBS 3:26 NKJV

I am confident of this very thing, that He who began a good
work in you will perfect it until the day of Christ Jesus.

PHILIPPIANS 1:6 NASB

Let us then approach God's throne of grace with confidence,
so that we may receive mercy and find grace to help us in our
time of need.

HEBREWS 4:16 NIV

This is the confidence that we have in Him, that if we ask
anything according to His will, He hears us. And if we know
that He hears us, whatever we ask, we know that we have the
petitions that we have asked of Him.

1 JOHN 5:14–15 NKJV

Contentment

To enjoy your work and to accept your lot in life—
that is indeed a gift from God. The person who does
that will not need to look back with sorrow on his past,
for God gives him joy.

ECCLESIASTES 5:20 TLB

I know what it is to be in need, and I know what it is to have
plenty. I have learned the secret of being content in any and
every situation, whether well fed or hungry, whether living in
plenty or in want. I can do all this through him who gives me
strength.

PHILIPPIANS 4:12-13 NIV

"If God cares so wonderfully for wildflowers that are here
today and thrown into the fire tomorrow, he will certainly care
for you. Why do you have so little faith? So don't worry about
these things, saying, 'What will we eat? What will we drink?
What will we wear?' These things dominate the thoughts of
unbelievers, but your heavenly Father already knows all your
needs. Seek the Kingdom of God above all else, and live
righteously, and he will give you everything you need."

MATTHEW 6:30-33 NLT

Courage

When I am afraid, I put my trust in you.
In God, whose word I praise—
in God I trust and am not afraid.

PSALM 56:3–4 NIV

Be on guard. Stand firm in the faith. Be courageous.
Be strong. And do everything with love.

1 CORINTHIANS 16:13–14 NLT

Be strong and courageous. Do not be frightened,
and do not be dismayed, for the LORD your God
is with you wherever you go.

JOSHUA 1:9 ESV

Love the LORD, all you godly ones!
For the LORD protects those who are loyal to him,
but he harshly punishes the arrogant.
So be strong and courageous,
all you who put your hope in the LORD!

PSALM 31:23–24 NLT

Be strong in the Lord and in his mighty power.
Put on the full armor of God, so that you can
take your stand against the devil's schemes.

EPHESIANS 6:10–11 NIV

Even though I walk through the valley
of the shadow of death,
I fear no evil, for You are with me;
Your rod and Your staff, they comfort me.

PSALM 23:4 NASB

Delight

The LORD directs the steps of the godly.
He delights in every detail of their lives.
Though they stumble, they will never fall,
for the LORD holds them by the hand.

PSALM 37:23–24 NLT

"He tends his flock like a shepherd:
He gathers the lambs in his arms
and carries them close to his heart;
he gently leads those that have young."

ISAIAH 40:11 NIV

I am sure that neither death nor life, nor angels nor rulers, nor
things present nor things to come, nor powers, nor height
nor depth, nor anything else in all creation, will be able to
separate us from the love of God in Christ Jesus our Lord.

ROMANS 8:38–39 ESV

Blessed be the LORD,
Because He has heard the voice of my supplication.
The LORD is my strength and my shield;
My heart trusts in Him, and I am helped;
Therefore my heart exults,
And with my song I shall thank Him.

PSALM 28:6-7 NASB

Depression

Why, my soul, are you downcast?
Why so disturbed within me?
Put your hope in God,
for I will yet praise him,
my Savior and my God.

PSALM 42:11 NIV

You are a chosen people, a royal priesthood, a holy nation, God's special possession, that you may declare the praises of him who called you out of darkness into his wonderful light.

1 PETER 2:9 NIV

He has delivered us from the power of darkness and conveyed us into the kingdom of the Son of His love.

COLOSSIANS 1:13 NKJV

You, O LORD, are a shield about me,
my glory, and the lifter of my head.

PSALM 3:3 ESV

The LORD is good to those whose hope is in him,
to the one who seeks him.

LAMENTATIONS 3:25 NIV

Unfailing love surrounds those who trust the LORD.
So rejoice in the LORD and be glad, all you who obey him!
Shout for joy, all you whose hearts are pure!

PSALM 32:10-11 NLT

Diligence

The plans of the diligent lead to profit
as surely as haste leads to poverty.

PROVERBS 21:5 NIV

In all the work you are doing, work the best you can.
Work as if you were doing it for the Lord, not for people.

COLOSSIANS 3:23 NCV

Be diligent in these matters; give yourself wholly to them,
so that everyone may see your progress.

1 TIMOTHY 4:15 NIV

Each of you should use whatever gift you have received to
serve others, as faithful stewards of God's grace in its various
forms. If anyone serves, they should do so with the strength
God provides, so that in all things God may be praised
through Jesus Christ.

1 PETER 4:10–11 NIV

Finish the work, so that your eager willingness to do it may
be matched by your completion of it, according to your
means.

2 CORINTHIANS 8:11 NIV

Pay careful attention to your own work, for then you will
get the satisfaction of a job well done, and you won't
need to compare yourself to anyone else. For we are each
responsible for our own conduct.

GALATIANS 6:4–5 NLT

Encouragement

Let everything you say be good and helpful, so that your words will be an encouragement to those who hear them.

EPHESIANS 4:29 NLT

Let us consider how to stir up one another to love and good works, not neglecting to meet together, as is the habit of some, but encouraging one another.

HEBREWS 10:24–25 ESV

For momentary, light affliction is producing for us an eternal weight of glory far beyond all comparison.

2 CORINTHIANS 4:17 NASB

The humble will see their God at work and be glad.
Let all who seek God's help be encouraged.

PSALM 69:32 NLT

We ask God to give you complete knowledge of his will and to give you spiritual wisdom and understanding. Then the way you live will always honor and please the Lord, and your lives will produce every kind of good fruit. All the while, you will grow as you learn to know God better and better.

COLOSSIANS 1:9–10 NLT

Enthusiasm

Whatever you do, work heartily, as for the Lord and not for men, knowing that from the Lord you will receive the inheritance as your reward. You are serving the Lord Christ.

COLOSSIANS 3:23–24 ESV

"When I discovered your words, I devoured them.
They are my joy and my heart's delight,
for I bear your name,
O LORD God of Heaven's Armies."

JEREMIAH 15:16 NLT

Make the most of every opportunity. Let your conversation be always full of grace.

COLOSSIANS 4:5–6 NIV

You will light my lamp;
The LORD my God will enlighten my darkness.
For by You I can run against a troop,
By my God I can leap over a wall.

PSALM 18:28–29 NKJV

It is a wonderful thing to be alive! If a person lives to be very old, let him rejoice in every day of life, but let him also remember that eternity is far longer and that everything down here is futile in comparison.

ECCLESIASTES 11:7–8 TLB

Excellence

"Many women have done excellently,
but you surpass them all."
Charm is deceitful, and beauty is vain,
but a woman who fears the LORD is to be praised.
Give her of the fruit of her hands,
and let her works praise her in the gates.

PROVERBS 31:29–31 ESV

It is my prayer that your love may abound more and more,
with knowledge and all discernment, so that you may
approve what is excellent, and so be pure and blameless for
the day of Christ.

PHILIPPIANS 1:9–10 ESV

His divine power has granted to us everything pertaining to
life and godliness, through the true knowledge of Him who
called us by His own glory and excellence.

2 PETER 1:3 NASB

Whether you eat or drink, or whatever you do, do all to the
glory of God.

1 CORINTHIANS 10:31 NKJV

Do your best to present yourself to God as one approved,
a worker who does not need to be ashamed and who
correctly handles the word of truth.

2 TIMOTHY 2:15 NIV

Faith

Faith is confidence in what we hope for and assurance about what we do not see.

HEBREWS 11:1 NIV

"If you have faith like a grain of mustard seed, you will say to this mountain, 'Move from here to there,' and it will move, and nothing will be impossible for you."

MATTHEW 17:20 ESV

Without faith it is impossible to please God, because anyone who comes to him must believe that he exists and that he rewards those who earnestly seek him.

HEBREWS 11:6 NIV

Faith comes by hearing, and hearing by the word of God.

ROMANS 10:17 NKJV

As we pray to our God and Father about you, we think of your faithful work, your loving deeds, and the enduring hope you have because of our Lord Jesus Christ.

1 THESSALONIANS 1:3 NLT

Through Christ you have come to trust in God. And you have placed your faith and hope in God because he raised Christ from the dead and gave him great glory.

1 PETER 1:21 NLT

Faithfulness

LORD, you are my God;
I will exalt you and praise your name,
for in perfect faithfulness
you have done wonderful things,
things planned long ago.

ISAIAH 25:1 NIV

I will sing of the LORD's great love forever;
with my mouth I will make your faithfulness known
through all generations.
I will declare that your love stands firm forever,
that you have established your faithfulness in heaven itself.

PSALM 89:1–2 NIV

God is faithful. He will not allow the temptation to be more
than you can stand. When you are tempted, he will show you
a way out so that you can endure.

1 CORINTHIANS 10:13 NLT

Your lovingkindness, O LORD, extends to the heavens,
Your faithfulness reaches to the skies.

PSALM 36:5 NASB

The word of the LORD is upright,
and all his work is done in faithfulness.

PSALM 33:4 ESV

The steadfast love of the LORD never ceases;
his mercies never come to an end;
they are new every morning;
great is your faithfulness.

LAMENTATIONS 3:22–23 ESV

Family

"Choose for yourselves this day whom you will serve...
as for me and my household, we will serve the Lord."

JOSHUA 24:15 NIV

Her children arise and call her blessed;
her husband also, and he praises her.

PROVERBS 31:28 NIV

Wives, submit to your husbands, as is fitting for those who
belong to the Lord. Husbands, love your wives and never
treat them harshly. Children, always obey your parents, for
this pleases the Lord.

COLOSSIANS 3:18-20 NLT

Be kindly affectionate to one another with brotherly love,
in honor giving preference to one another.

ROMANS 12:10 NKJV

Be like-minded, be sympathetic, love one another,
be compassionate and humble.

1 PETER 3:8 NIV

Live wisely among those who are not believers, and make the
most of every opportunity. Let your conversation be gracious
and attractive so that you will have the right response for
everyone.

COLOSSIANS 4:5-6 NLT

For this reason I bow my knees before the Father, from whom
every family in heaven and on earth derives its name.

EPHESIANS 3:14-15 NASB

Fear

God has not given us a spirit of fear,
but of power and of love and of a sound mind.

2 Timothy 1:7 nkjv

When you lie down, you will not be afraid;
when you lie down, your sleep will be sweet.

Proverbs 3:24 niv

The name of the Lord is a strong tower;
The righteous runs into it and is safe.

Proverbs 18:10 nasb

God is our refuge and strength,
an ever-present help in trouble.

Psalm 46:1 niv

Where God's love is, there is no fear, because God's perfect
love drives out fear. It is punishment that makes a person
fear, so love is not made perfect in the person who fears.

1 John 4:18 ncv

"Don't be afraid, for I am with you.
Don't be discouraged, for I am your God.
I will strengthen you and help you.
I will hold you up with my victorious right hand."

Isaiah 41:10 nlt

The Lord is my light and my salvation;
whom shall I fear?
The Lord is the stronghold of my life;
of whom shall I be afraid?

Psalm 27:1 esv

Finances

Don't love money; be satisfied with what you have.
For God has said, "I will never fail you.
I will never abandon you."

HEBREWS 13:5 NLT

My God will meet all your needs according to the riches of
his glory in Christ Jesus.

PHILIPPIANS 4:19 NIV

With me are riches and honor,
enduring wealth and prosperity.
My fruit is better than fine gold;
what I yield surpasses choice silver.
I walk in the way of righteousness,
along the paths of justice,
bestowing a rich inheritance on those who love me
and making their treasuries full.

PROVERBS 8:18–21 NIV

"Whoever wishes to save his life will lose it; but whoever
loses his life for My sake will find it. For what will it profit
a man if he gains the whole world and forfeits his soul?
Or what will a man give in exchange for his soul?"

MATTHEW 16:25–26 NASB

As for the rich in this present age, charge them not to be
haughty, nor to set their hopes on the uncertainty of riches,
but on God, who richly provides us with everything to enjoy.

1 TIMOTHY 6:17 ESV

Flexibility

You are our Father;
We are the clay, and You our potter;
And all we are the work of Your hand.

ISAIAH 64:8 NKJV

I know how to be brought low, and I know how to abound.
In any and every circumstance, I have learned the secret of
facing plenty and hunger, abundance and need. I can do all
things through him who strengthens me.

PHILIPPIANS 4:12–13 ESV

Happy are those who listen to me,
watching at my door every day,
waiting at my open doorway.
Those who find me find life,
and the LORD will be pleased with them.

PROVERBS 8:34–35 NCV

Accept other believers...and don't argue with them about
what they think is right or wrong. For instance...those who
worship the Lord on a special day do it to honor him. Those
who eat any kind of food do so to honor the Lord, since they
give thanks to God before eating. And those who refuse
to eat certain foods also want to please the Lord and give
thanks to God.

ROMANS 14:1–2, 6 NLT

Forgiveness

He is so rich in kindness and grace that he purchased our freedom with the blood of his Son and forgave our sins.

EPHESIANS 1:7 NLT

As far as the east is from the west,
So far has He removed our transgressions from us.

PSALM 103:12 NASB

If we confess our sins, He is faithful and just to forgive us our sins and to cleanse us from all unrighteousness.

1 JOHN 1:9 NKJV

"If you forgive other people when they sin against you, your heavenly Father will also forgive you."

MATTHEW 6:14 NIV

My sacrifice, O God, is a broken spirit;
a broken and contrite heart you, God, will not despise.

PSALM 51:17 NIV

"Whenever you stand praying, forgive, if you have anything against anyone, so that your Father also who is in heaven may forgive you."

MARK 11:25 ESV

For You, Lord, are good, and ready to forgive,
And abundant in mercy to all those who call upon You.

PSALM 86:5 NKJV

"Her sins—and they are many—have been forgiven, so she has shown me much love. But a person who is forgiven little shows only little love."

LUKE 7:47 NLT

Friendship

There are "friends" who pretend to be friends,
but there is a friend who sticks closer than a brother.

PROVERBS 18:24 TLB

"Greater love has no one than this: to lay down one's life for
one's friends. You are my friends if you do what I command.
I no longer call you servants, because a servant does not
know his master's business. Instead, I have called you friends,
for everything that I learned from my Father I have made
known to you."

JOHN 15:13–15 NIV

Love prospers when a fault is forgiven,
but dwelling on it separates close friends.

PROVERBS 17:9 NLT

"Do to others whatever you would like them to do to you.
This is the essence of all that is taught in the law
and the prophets."

MATTHEW 7:12 NLT

Like an earring of gold or an ornament of fine gold
is the rebuke of a wise judge to a listening ear.
Like a snow-cooled drink at harvest time
is a trustworthy messenger to the one who sends him.

PROVERBS 25:12–13 NIV

A friend loves at all times.

PROVERBS 17:17 NKJV

Generosity

One person gives freely, yet gains even more;
another withholds unduly, but comes to poverty.
A generous person will prosper;
whoever refreshes others will be refreshed.

PROVERBS 11:24–25 NIV

Let each one give as he purposes in his heart, not grudgingly
or of necessity; for God loves a cheerful giver.

2 CORINTHIANS 9:7 NKJV

The generous will themselves be blessed,
for they share their food with the poor.

PROVERBS 22:9 NIV

Whoever is generous to the poor lends to the LORD,
and he will repay him for his deed.

PROVERBS 19:17 ESV

"When you give to the needy, do not let your left hand know
what your right hand is doing, so that your giving may be in
secret. Then your Father, who sees what is done in secret, will
reward you."

MATTHEW 6:3–4 NIV

You shall generously give to him, and your heart shall not
be grieved when you give to him, because for this thing
 the LORD your God will bless you in all your work
and in all your undertakings.

DEUTERONOMY 15:10 NASB

It is more blessed to give than to receive.

ACTS 20:35 NIV

Gentleness

"Blessed are the gentle, for they shall inherit the earth."

MATTHEW 5:5 NASB

A gentle answer turns away wrath,
but a harsh word stirs up anger.

PROVERBS 15:1 NIV

It is not fancy hair, gold jewelry, or fine clothes that should make you beautiful. No, your beauty should come from within you—the beauty of a gentle and quiet spirit that will never be destroyed and is very precious to God.

1 PETER 3:3-4 NCV

The wisdom that is from above is first pure, then peaceable, gentle, willing to yield, full of mercy and good fruits, without partiality and without hypocrisy.

JAMES 3:17 NKJV

If anyone is caught in any trespass… restore such a one in a spirit of gentleness; each one looking to yourself, so that you too will not be tempted.

GALATIANS 6:1 NASB

"Take my yoke upon you, and learn from me, for I am gentle and lowly in heart, and you will find rest for your souls."

MATTHEW 11:29 ESV

Goodness

Everything God created is good, and nothing is to be rejected if it is received with thanksgiving.

1 Timothy 4:4 NIV

Examine everything carefully; hold fast to that which is good; abstain from every form of evil.

1 Thessalonians 5:21-22 NASB

The Lord is good to all,
and his mercy is over all that he has made.

Psalm 145:9 ESV

How great is the goodness
you have stored up for those who fear you.
You lavish it on those who come to you for protection,
blessing them before the watching world.

Psalm 31:19 NLT

Work with enthusiasm, as though you were working for the Lord rather than for people. Remember that the Lord will reward each one of us for the good we do.

Ephesians 6:7–8 NLT

"A good man's speech reveals the rich treasures within him."

Matthew 12:35 TLB

Praise the Lord!
Oh, give thanks to the Lord, for He is good!
For His mercy endures forever.

Psalm 106:1 NKJV

Grace

God is so rich in mercy, and he loved us so much, that even though we were dead because of our sins, he gave us life when he raised Christ from the dead. (It is only by God's grace that you have been saved!)… God saved you by his grace when you believed. And you can't take credit for this; it is a gift from God. Salvation is not a reward for the good things we have done, so none of us can boast about it.

EPHESIANS 2:4–5, 8–9 NLT

The Ten Commandments were given so that all could see the extent of their failure to obey God's laws. But the more we see our sinfulness, the more we see God's abounding grace forgiving us. Before, sin ruled over all men and brought them to death, but now God's kindness rules instead, giving us right standing with God and resulting in eternal life through Jesus Christ our Lord.

ROMANS 5:20–21 TLB

Sin shall no longer be your master, because you are not under the law, but under grace.

ROMANS 6:14 NIV

Grief

To all who mourn...he will give: beauty for ashes; joy instead of mourning; praise instead of heaviness. For God has planted them like strong and graceful oaks for his own glory.

ISAIAH 61:3 TLB

Blessed be the God...of all comfort, who comforts us in all our tribulation, that we may be able to comfort those who are in any trouble, with the comfort with which we ourselves are comforted by God.

2 CORINTHIANS 1:3–4 NKJV

He turned my sorrow into joy! He took away my clothes of mourning and clothed me with joy.

PSALM 30:11 TLB

Those that the LORD has rescued will return.
They will enter Zion with singing;
everlasting joy will crown their heads.
Gladness and joy will overtake them,
and sorrow and sighing will flee away.

ISAIAH 35:10 NIV

"He will once again fill your mouth with laughter
and your lips with shouts of joy."

JOB 8:21 NLT

May our Lord Jesus Christ himself and God our Father, who loved us and by his grace gave us eternal comfort and a wonderful hope, comfort you and strengthen you.

2 THESSALONIANS 2:16–17 NLT

Guidance

I will instruct you and teach you in the way you should go;
I will counsel you with my loving eye on you.

PSALM 32:8 NIV

We can make our plans,
but the LORD determines our steps.

PROVERBS 16:9 NLT

Listen to advice and accept discipline,
and at the end you will be counted among the wise.

PROVERBS 19:20 NIV

Guide me in your truth and teach me,
for you are God my Savior,
and my hope is in you all day long.

PSALM 25:5 NIV

Trust in the LORD with all your heart,
And lean not on your own understanding;
In all your ways acknowledge Him,
And He shall direct your paths.

PROVERBS 3:5–6 NKJV

Whether you turn to the right or to the left,
your ears will hear a voice behind you, saying,
"This is the way; walk in it."

ISAIAH 30:21 NIV

The true children of God are those who let God's Spirit lead
them.

ROMANS 8:14 NCV

Guilt

Since we have a great High Priest who rules over God's house, let us go right into the presence of God with sincere hearts fully trusting him. For our guilty consciences have been sprinkled with Christ's blood to make us clean, and our bodies have been washed with pure water.

HEBREWS 10:21-22 NLT

"Very truly I tell you, whoever hears my word and believes him who sent me has eternal life and will not be judged but has crossed over from death to life."

JOHN 5:24 NIV

"I am the One who erases all your sins, for my sake; I will not remember your sins."

ISAIAH 43:25 NCV

"God did not send his Son into the world to condemn the world, but to save the world through him. Whoever believes in him is not condemned, but whoever does not believe stands condemned already because they have not believed in the name of God's one and only Son."

JOHN 3:17-18 NIV

Therefore, there is now no condemnation for those who are in Christ Jesus, because through Christ Jesus the law of the Spirit who gives life has set you free from the law of sin and death.

ROMANS 8:1-2 NIV

Health

A cheerful heart does good like medicine.

PROVERBS 17:22 TLB

My child, pay attention to what I say.
Listen carefully to my words.
Don't lose sight of them.
Let them penetrate deep into your heart,
for they bring life to those who find them,
and healing to their whole body.

PROVERBS 4:20–22 NLT

He was pierced for our transgressions,
he was crushed for our iniquities;
the punishment that brought us peace was on him,
and by his wounds we are healed.

ISAIAH 53:5 NIV

Trust the LORD with all your heart,
and don't depend on your own understanding.
Remember the LORD in all you do,
and he will give you success.
Don't depend on your own wisdom.
Respect the LORD and refuse to do wrong.
Then your body will be healthy,
and your bones will be strong.

PROVERBS 3:5-6 NCV

The world and its desires pass away,
but whoever does the will of God lives forever.

1 JOHN 2:17 NIV

Helpfulness

Give generously, for your gifts will return to you later.
Divide your gifts among many, for in the days ahead
you yourself may need much help.

ECCLESIASTES 11:1–2 TLB

God has given each of you a gift from his great variety of
spiritual gifts. Use them well to serve one another.

1 PETER 4:10 NLT

"Who is the greater, one who reclines at table or one who
serves? Is it not the one who reclines at table? But I am
among you as the one who serves."

LUKE 22:27 ESV

"Even the Son of Man did not come to be served,
but to serve, and to give His life a ransom for many."

MARK 10:45 NKJV

Let the message about Christ, in all its richness, fill your
lives. Teach and counsel each other with all the wisdom he
gives. Sing psalms and hymns and spiritual songs to God
with thankful hearts. And whatever you do or say, do it as a
representative of the Lord Jesus, giving thanks through him
to God the Father.

COLOSSIANS 3:16–17 NLT

Heritage

The Lord is the portion of my inheritance and my cup;
You support my lot.
The lines have fallen to me in pleasant places;
Indeed, my heritage is beautiful to me.

PSALM 16:5-6

Children are a heritage from the Lord,
offspring a reward from him.

PSALM 127:3 NIV

Let the message of Christ dwell among you richly as you
teach and admonish one another with all wisdom through
psalms, hymns, and songs from the Spirit, singing to God
with gratitude in your hearts.

COLOSSIANS 3:16 NIV

"So commit yourselves wholeheartedly to these words of
mine. Tie them to your hands and wear them on your forehead
as reminders. Teach them to your children. Talk about them
when you are at home and when you are on the road, when
you are going to bed and when you are getting up."

DEUTERONOMY 11:18-19 NLT

I will sing of the mercies of the Lord forever;
With my mouth will I make known Your faithfulness to all
generations.

PSALM 8:9 1 NKJV

Hope

We can rejoice, too, when we run into problems and trials, for we know that they help us develop endurance. And endurance develops strength of character, and character strengthens our confident hope of salvation. And this hope will not lead to disappointment. For we know how dearly God loves us, because he has given us the Holy Spirit to fill our hearts with his love.

ROMANS 5:3–5 NLT

He lifts the poor from the dust
and the needy from the garbage dump.
He sets them among princes,
placing them in seats of honor.
For all the earth is the LORD's,
and he has set the world in order.

1 SAMUEL 2:7–8 NLT

May the God of hope fill you with all joy and peace as you trust in him, so that you may overflow with hope by the power of the Holy Spirit.

ROMANS 15:13 NIV

Blessed be the God and Father of our Lord Jesus Christ! According to his great mercy, he has caused us to be born again to a living hope through the resurrection of Jesus Christ.

1 PETER 1:3 ESV

Humility

Be humble under God's powerful hand so he will lift you up when the right time comes.

1 Peter 5:6 ncv

The Lord has told you what is good,
and this is what he requires of you:
to do what is right, to love mercy,
and to walk humbly with your God.

Micah 6:8 nlt

Humble yourselves in the sight of the Lord,
and He will lift you up.

James 4:10 nkjv

In your relationships with one another, have the same
mindset as Christ Jesus:
Who, being in very nature God,
did not consider equality with God something
to be used to his own advantage;
rather, he made himself nothing
by taking the very nature of a servant,
being made in human likeness.
And being found in appearance as a man,
he humbled himself
by becoming obedient to death—
even death on a cross!
Therefore God exalted him to the highest place
and gave him the name that is above every name.

Philippians 2:5–9 niv

Identity

See how very much our Father loves us, for he calls us his children, and that is what we are! But the people who belong to this world don't recognize that we are God's children because they don't know him. Dear friends, we are already God's children, but he has not yet shown us what we will be like when Christ appears. But we do know that we will be like him, for we will see him as he really is.

1 JOHN 3:1-2 NLT

Do everything without grumbling or arguing, so that you may become blameless and pure, "children of God without fault in a warped and crooked generation." Then you will shine among them like stars in the sky as you hold firmly to the word of life.

PHILIPPIANS 2:14-16 NIV

I have been crucified with Christ; and it is no longer I who live, but Christ lives in me; and the life which I now live in the flesh I live by faith in the Son of God, who loved me and gave Himself up for me.

GALATIANS 2:20 NASB

Inspiration

The precepts of the Lord are right,
giving joy to the heart.
The commands of the Lord are radiant,
giving light to the eyes.

PSALM 19:8 NIV

"I am the Light of the world; he who follows Me will not walk in the darkness, but will have the Light of life."

JOHN 8:12 NASB

"You are the light of the world. A city set on a hill cannot be hidden. Nor do people light a lamp and put it under a basket, but on a stand, and it gives light to all in the house. In the same way, let your light shine before others, so that they may see your good works and give glory to your Father who is in heaven."

MATTHEW 5:14–16 ESV

Live in the right way, serve God, have faith, love, patience, and gentleness. Fight the good fight of faith, grabbing hold of the life that continues forever. You were called to have that life when you confessed the good confession before many witnesses.

1 TIMOTHY 6:11–12 NCV

Your laws are my treasure; they are my heart's delight.

PSALM 119:111 NLT

Intimacy

God's solid foundation stands firm, sealed with this inscription: "The Lord knows those who are his."

2 TIMOTHY 2:19 NIV

When I was a child, I spoke and thought and reasoned as a child. But when I grew up, I put away childish things. Now we see things imperfectly, like puzzling reflections in a mirror, but then we will see everything with perfect clarity. All that I know now is partial and incomplete, but then I will know everything completely, just as God now knows me completely.

1 CORINTHIANS 13:11-12 NLT

"For I know the plans I have for you," declares the LORD,
"plans to prosper you and not to harm you,
plans to give you hope and a future."

JEREMIAH 29:11 NIV

O LORD, You have searched me and known me.
You know my sitting down and my rising up;
You understand my thought afar off.
You comprehend my path and my lying down,
And are acquainted with all my ways.
For there is not a word on my tongue,
But behold, O LORD, You know it altogether.

PSALM 139:1–4 NKJV

Joy

"Until now you have not asked for anything in my name.
Ask and you will receive, and your joy will be complete."

JOHN 16:24 NIV

"You will go out in joy
and be led forth in peace;
the mountains and hills
will burst into song before you,
and all the trees of the field
will clap their hands."

ISAIAH 55:12 NIV

"I have told you this so that my joy may be in you and that
your joy may be complete."

JOHN 15:11 NIV

Let all those rejoice who put their trust in You;
Let them ever shout for joy, because You defend them;
Let those also who love Your name
Be joyful in You.

PSALM 5:11 NKJV

Our mouth was filled with laughter,
and our tongue with shouts of joy.

PSALM 126:2 ESV

Be truly glad! There is wonderful joy ahead.... You love him
even though you have never seen him. Though you do not
see him now, you trust him; and you rejoice with a glorious,
inexpressible joy.

1 PETER 1:6, 8 NLT

Justice

He did not retaliate when he was insulted, nor threaten revenge when he suffered. He left his case in the hands of God, who always judges fairly.

1 PETER 2:23 NLT

"Look, I am coming soon! My reward is with me, and I will give to each person according to what they have done."

REVELATION 22:12 NIV

The LORD secures justice for the poor
and upholds the cause of the needy.

PSALM 140:12 NIV

Beloved, do not avenge yourselves, but rather give place to wrath; for it is written, "Vengeance is Mine, I will repay," says the Lord.

ROMANS 12:19 NKJV

Righteousness and justice are the foundation of Your throne.

PSALM 89:14 NKJV

"Seek justice, correct oppression; bring justice to the fatherless, plead the widow's cause."

ISAIAH 1:17 ESV

He will not judge by appearance, false evidence, or hearsay, but will defend the poor and the exploited. He will rule against the wicked who oppress them. For he will be clothed with fairness and with truth.

ISAIAH 11:3–5 TLB

Kindness

His merciful kindness is great toward us,
And the truth of the LORD endures forever.
Praise the LORD!

PSALM 117:2 NKJV

When she speaks, her words are wise,
and she gives instructions with kindness.

PROVERBS 31:26 NLT

How does God's love abide in anyone who has the world's
goods and sees a brother or sister in need and yet refuses
help? Little children, let us love, not in word or speech, but in
truth and action.

1 JOHN 3:17–18 NRSV

"Love your enemies, do good to them, and lend to them
without expecting to get anything back. Then your reward
will be great, and you will be children of the Most High."

LUKE 6:35 NIV

Do you presume on the riches of his kindness and
forbearance and patience, not knowing that God's kindness
is meant to lead you to repentance?

ROMANS 2:4 ESV

I will tell of the kindnesses of the LORD,
the deeds for which he is to be praised...
according to his compassion and many kindnesses.

ISAIAH 63:7 NIV

Be kind and compassionate to one another.

EPHESIANS 4:32 NIV

Loneliness

The LORD is near to all who call on him,
to all who call on him in truth.

PSALM 145:18 NIV

I fall to my knees and pray to the Father, the Creator of everything in heaven and on earth. I pray that from his glorious, unlimited resources he will empower you with inner strength through his Spirit. Then Christ will make his home in your hearts as you trust in him. Your roots will grow down into God's love and keep you strong. And may you have the power to understand, as all God's people should, how wide, how long, how high, and how deep his love is. May you experience the love of Christ, though it is too great to understand fully. Then you will be made complete with all the fullness of life and power that comes from God.

EPHESIANS 3:14–19 NLT

Turn to me and have mercy,
for I am alone and in deep distress.

PSALM 25:16 NLT

By this we know that we abide in Him and He in us, because He has given us of His Spirit.

1 JOHN 4:13 NASB

Love

Satisfy us in the morning with your unfailing love,
that we may sing for joy and be glad all our days.

PSALM 90:14 NIV

Three things will last forever—faith, hope, and love—
and the greatest of these is love.

1 CORINTHIANS 13:13 NLT

You, O Lord, are good and forgiving,
abounding in steadfast love to all who call upon you.

PSALM 86:5 ESV

"God loved the world so much that he gave his only Son so
that anyone who believes in him shall not perish but have
eternal life."

JOHN 3:16 TLB

Know therefore that the LORD your God is God;
he is the faithful God, keeping his covenant of love
to a thousand generations of those who love him
and keep his commandments.

DEUTERONOMY 7:9 NIV

Let love be without hypocrisy. Abhor what is evil. Cling to
what is good. Be kindly affectionate to one another with
brotherly love.

ROMANS 12:9–10 NKJV

Let love and faithfulness never leave you;
bind them around your neck,
write them on the tablet of your heart.

PROVERBS 3:3 NIV

Nourishment

Happy are those
who do not follow the advice of the wicked,
or take the path that sinners tread,
or sit in the seat of scoffers;
but their delight is in the law of the LORD,
and on his law they meditate day and night.
They are like trees
planted by streams of water,
which yield their fruit in its season,
and their leaves do not wither.
In all that they do, they prosper.

PSALM 1:1-3 NRSV

"My nourishment comes from doing the will of God, who sent me, and from finishing his work."

JOHN 4:34 NLT

"Abide in Me, and I in you. As the branch cannot bear fruit of itself, unless it abides in the vine, neither can you, unless you abide in Me. I am the vine, you are the branches. He who abides in Me, and I in him, bears much fruit; for without Me you can do nothing."

JOHN 15:4-5 NKJV

Jesus said to them, "I am the bread of life;
whoever comes to me shall not hunger,
and whoever believes in me shall never thirst."

JOHN 6:35 ESV

Patience

They who wait for the LORD
shall renew their strength;
they shall mount up with wings like eagles;
they shall run and not be weary;
they shall walk and not faint.

ISAIAH 40:31 ESV

May the God of endurance and encouragement grant you to live in such harmony with one another.

ROMANS 15:5–7 ESV

Have unity of spirit, sympathy, love for one another, a tender heart, and a humble mind. Do not repay evil for evil or abuse for abuse; but, on the contrary, repay with a blessing. It is for this that you were called—that you might inherit a blessing.

1 PETER 3:8–9 NRSV

Follow the example of those who are going to inherit God's promises because of their faith and endurance.

HEBREWS 6:12 NLT

Make me truly happy by agreeing wholeheartedly with each other, loving one another, and working together with one mind and purpose.

PHILIPPIANS 2:2 NLT

Live in harmony with one another. Do not be proud,
but be willing to associate with people of low position.
Do not be conceited.

ROMANS 12:16 NIV

Peace

"Peace I leave with you; my peace I give you. I do not give to you as the world gives. Do not let your hearts be troubled and do not be afraid."

JOHN 14:27 NIV

Those who love your instructions have great peace and do not stumble.

PSALM 119:165 NLT

If their thinking is controlled by the Spirit, there is life and peace.

ROMANS 8:6 NCV

God is not a God of confusion but of peace.

1 CORINTHIANS 14:33 NASB

The LORD will give strength to His people;
The LORD will bless His people with peace.

PSALM 29:11 NKJV

Let the peace of Christ rule in your hearts, since as members of one body you were called to peace.

COLOSSIANS 3:15 NIV

"These things I have spoken to you, so that in Me you may have peace. In the world you have tribulation, but take courage; I have overcome the world."

JOHN 16:33 NASB

May the Lord of peace himself give you peace at all times and in every way. The Lord be with all of you.

2 THESSALONIANS 3:16 NIV

Perseverance

Let us not grow weary of doing good, for in due season we will reap, if we do not give up.

GALATIANS 6:9 ESV

Consider it pure joy...whenever you face trials of many kinds, because you know that the testing of your faith develops perseverance. Perseverance must finish its work so that you may be mature and complete, not lacking anything.

JAMES 1:2–4 NIV

May the Lord direct your hearts into God's love and Christ's perseverance.

2 THESSALONIANS 3:5 NIV

God blesses those who patiently endure testing and temptation. Afterward they will receive the crown of life that God has promised to those who love him.

JAMES 1:12 NLT

Let us run with perseverance the race marked out for us, fixing our eyes on Jesus, the pioneer and perfecter of faith. For the joy set before him he endured the cross, scorning its shame, and sat down at the right hand of the throne of God. Consider him who endured such opposition from sinners, so that you will not grow weary and lose heart.

HEBREWS 12:1–3 NIV

Praise

Praise the LORD!
Praise God in his sanctuary;
praise him in his mighty heavens!
Praise him for his mighty deeds;
praise him according to his excellent greatness!...
Let everything that has breath praise the LORD!

PSALM 150:1–2, 6 ESV

Let us continually offer the sacrifice of praise to God, that is,
the fruit of our lips, giving thanks to His name.

HEBREWS 13:15 NKJV

O LORD, You are my God.
I will exalt You,
I will praise Your name,
For You have done wonderful things.

ISAIAH 25:1 NKJV

Praise the LORD from the heavens;
praise him in the heights above.
Praise him, all his angels;
praise him, all his heavenly hosts.
Praise him, sun and moon;
praise him, all you shining stars.
Praise him, you highest heavens
and you waters above the skies.
Let them praise the name of the LORD,
for at his command they were created.

PSALM 148:1–5 NIV

Prayer

Pray without ceasing.

1 Thessalonians 5:17 NKJV

"Ask and it will be given to you; seek and you will find; knock and the door will be opened to you. For everyone who asks receives; he who seeks finds; and to him who knocks, the door will be opened."

Matthew 7:7–8 NIV

My voice You shall hear in the morning, O Lord;
In the morning I will direct it to You,
And I will look up.

Psalm 5:3 NKJV

Confess your sins to each other and pray for each other so that you may be healed. The prayer of a righteous person is powerful and effective.

James 5:16 NIV

You, God, are my God, earnestly I seek you;
I thirst for you, my whole being longs for you,
in a dry and parched land where there is no water.

Psalm 63:1 NIV

Pray about everything. Tell God what you need, and thank him for all he has done.

Philippians 4:6 NLT

The Spirit also helps our weakness; for we do not know how to pray as we should, but the Spirit Himself intercedes for us with groanings too deep for words.

Romans 8:26 NASB

Promises

He has granted to us his precious and very great promises, so that through them you may become partakers of the divine nature, having escaped from the corruption that is in the world.

2 PETER 1:3-4 ESV

Your promises have been thoroughly tested,
and your servant loves them.
…My eyes stay open through the watches of the night,
that I may meditate on your promises.

PSALM 119:140, 148 NIV

All of God's promises have been fulfilled in Christ with a resounding "Yes!"

2 CORINTHIANS 1:20 NLT

To him who is able to do immeasurably more than all we ask or imagine, according to his power that is at work within us, to him be glory...for ever and ever! Amen.

EPHESIANS 3:20–21 NIV

The LORD always keeps his promises;
he is gracious in all he does.

PSALM 145:13 NLT

Not one word of all the good words which the LORD your God spoke concerning you has failed; all have been fulfilled for you, not one of them has failed.

JOSHUA 23:14 NASB

Protection

The LORD hears his people
when they call to him for help.
He rescues them from all their troubles.

PSALM 34:17 NLT

You, God, see the trouble of the afflicted;
you consider their grief and take it in hand.
The victims commit themselves to you;
you are the helper of the fatherless.

PSALM 10:14 NIV

So we do not lose heart. Though our outer self is wasting
away, our inner self is being renewed day by day.

2 CORINTHIANS 4:16 ESV

You, O LORD, are a shield about me,
My glory, and the One who lifts my head.

PSALM 3:3 NASB

The LORD is near to the brokenhearted
and saves the crushed in spirit.

PSALM 34:18 ESV

LORD, you know the hopes of the helpless.
Surely you will hear their cries and comfort them.
You will bring justice to the orphans and the oppressed,
so mere people can no longer terrify them.

PSALM 10:17–18 NLT

Provision

All scripture is inspired by God and is useful for teaching, for reproof, for correction, and for training in righteousness, so that everyone who belongs to God may be proficient, equipped for every good work.

2 TIMOTHY 3:16–17 NRSV

May He give you the power to accomplish all the good things your faith prompts you to do.

2 THESSALONIANS 1:11 NLT

We are God's handiwork, created in Christ Jesus to do good works, which God prepared in advance for us to do.

EPHESIANS 2:10 NIV

Then the LORD reached out his hand and touched my mouth and said to me, "I have put my words in your mouth."

JEREMIAH 1:9 NIV

So then, my beloved, just as you have always obeyed, not as in my presence only, but now much more in my absence, work out your salvation with fear and trembling; for it is God who is at work in you, both to will and to work for His good pleasure.

PHILIPPIANS 2:12-13 NASB

Purpose

We know that all things work together for good to those who love God, to those who are the called according to His purpose.

ROMANS 8:28 NKJV

Live as citizens of heaven, conducting yourselves in a manner worthy of the Good News about Christ...standing together with one spirit and one purpose, fighting together for the faith. Don't be intimidated in any way by your enemies. This will be a sign to them that you are going to be saved, even by God himself.

PHILIPPIANS 1:27–28 NLT

Be attentive to my words;
incline your ear to my sayings.
Let them not escape from your sight;
keep them within your heart.
Let your eyes look directly forward,
and your gaze be straight before you.

PROVERBS 4:20–21, 25 ESV

If you have been raised with Christ, seek the things that are above, where Christ is, seated at the right hand of God. Set your minds on things that are above, not on things that are on earth, for you have died, and your life is hidden with Christ in God.

COLOSSIANS 3:1–3 NRSV

Refreshment

The law of the LORD is perfect,
refreshing the soul.
The statutes of the LORD are trustworthy,
making wise the simple.

PSALM 19:7 NIV

Jesus replied that people soon became thirsty again after drinking this water. "But the water I give them," he said, "becomes a perpetual spring within them, watering them forever with eternal life."

JOHN 4:13-14 TLB

Your love, LORD, reaches to the heavens,
your faithfulness to the skies.
Your righteousness is like the highest mountains,
your justice like the great deep.
People take refuge in the shadow of your wings.
They feast on the abundance of your house;
you give them drink from your river of delights.
For with you is the fountain of life;
in your light we see light.

PSALM 36:5–9 NIV

A generous person will prosper;
whoever refreshes others will be refreshed.

PROVERBS 11: 25 NIV

"Let anyone who is thirsty come to me and drink.
Whoever believes in me, as Scripture has said,
rivers of living water will flow from within them."

JOHN 7:37–38 NIV

Relationships

Two are better than one,
because they have a good return for their labor:
If either of them falls down,
one can help the other up.

ECCLESIASTES 4:9–10 NIV

Perfume and incense bring joy to the heart,
and the pleasantness of a friend
springs from their heartfelt advice.

PROVERBS 27:9 NIV

Love each other with genuine affection,
and take delight in honoring each other.

ROMANS 12:10 NLT

As those who have been chosen of God, holy and beloved,
put on a heart of compassion, kindness, humility, gentleness
and patience; bearing with one another, and forgiving each
other, whoever has a complaint against anyone; just as the
Lord forgave you, so also should you. Beyond all these things
put on love, which is the perfect bond of unity.

COLOSSIANS 3:12–14 NASB

As iron sharpens iron, so a friend sharpens a friend.

PROVERBS 27:17 NLT

Become complete. Be of good comfort, be of one mind, live
in peace; and the God of love and peace will be with you.

2 CORINTHIANS 13:11 NKJV

Reliability

You are near, LORD,
and all your commands are true.
Long ago I learned from your statutes
that you established them to last forever.

PSALM 119:151–152 NIV

Every good and perfect gift is from above, coming down
from the Father of the heavenly lights, who does not change
like shifting shadows.

JAMES 1:17 NIV

With all my heart I have sought You;
Do not let me wander from Your commandments.
Your word I have treasured in my heart,
That I may not sin against You.
…Teach me, O LORD, the way of Your statutes,
And I shall observe it to the end.

PSALM 119:10–11, 33 NASB

The grass withers,
And its flower falls away,
But the word of the LORD endures forever.

1 PETER 1:24–25 NKJV

"One who is faithful in a very little is also faithful in much."

LUKE 16:10 ESV

Watch yourselves, so that you may not lose what we have
worked for, but may win a full reward.

2 JOHN 1:8 ESV

Respect

Have confidence in your leaders and submit to their authority, because they keep watch over you as those who must give an account. Do this so that their work will be a joy, not a burden, for that would be of no benefit to you.

HEBREWS 13:17 NIV

Do nothing out of selfish ambition or vain conceit. Rather, in humility value others above yourselves, not looking to your own interests but each of you to the interests of the others.

PHILIPPIANS 2:3–4 NIV

Appreciate those who diligently labor among you, and have charge over you in the Lord and give you instruction...esteem them very highly in love because of their work. Live in peace with one another.

1 THESSALONIANS 5:12–13 NASB

For the Lord's sake, yield to the people who have authority in this world.... It is God's desire that by doing good you should stop foolish people from saying stupid things about you. Live as free people, but do not use your freedom as an excuse to do evil. Live as servants of God. Show respect for all people: Love the brothers and sisters of God's family.

1 PETER 2:13, 15–17 NCV

Reward

I have fought the good fight, I have finished the course, I have kept the faith; in the future there is laid up for me the crown of righteousness, which the Lord, the righteous Judge, will award to me on that day; and not only to me, but also to all who have loved His appearing.

2 TIMOTHY 4:7-8 NASB

Rest in the LORD and wait patiently for Him....
Those who wait for the LORD, they will inherit the land.

PSALM 37:7–9 NASB

Do not lose the courage you had in the past, which has a great reward. You must hold on, so you can do what God wants and receive what he has promised.

HEBREWS 10:35–36 NCV

Be on your guard, so that you do not lose what we have worked for, but may receive a full reward.

2 JOHN 1:8 NRSV

Wise words bring many benefits,
and hard work brings rewards.

PROVERBS 12:14 NLT

Satisfaction

Because your love is better than life,
my lips will glorify you.
I will praise you as long as I live,
and in your name I will lift up my hands.
I will be fully satisfied as with the richest of foods;
with singing lips my mouth will praise you.

PSALM 63:3–5 NIV

God is able to provide you with every blessing in abundance,
so that by always having enough of everything, you may
share abundantly in every good work.

2 CORINTHIANS 9:8 NRSV

The LORD is all I need.
He takes care of me.
My share in life has been pleasant;
my part has been beautiful.

PSALM 16:5–6 NCV

The poor shall eat and be satisfied; all who see the Lord shall
find him and shall praise his name. Their hearts shall rejoice
with everlasting joy.

PSALM 22:26 TLB

Give, and it will be given to you. A good measure,
pressed down, shaken together and running over,
will be poured into your lap.

LUKE 6:38 NIV

Whoever pursues righteousness and love
finds life, prosperity and honor.

PROVERBS 21:21 NIV

Self-control

The end of all things is at hand; therefore be self-controlled and sober-minded for the sake of your prayers.

1 Peter 4:7 esv

The grace of God has appeared that offers salvation to all people. It teaches us to say "No" to ungodliness and worldly passions, and to live self-controlled, upright and godly lives in this present age.

Titus 2:11-12 niv

Set a guard over my mouth, Lord;
keep watch over the door of my lips.
Do not let my heart be drawn to what is evil.

Psalm 141:3-4 niv

This is the will of God, your sanctification… that each one of you know how to control your own body in holiness and honor.

1 Thessalonians 4:3-4 nrsv

We all make many mistakes. For if we could control our tongues, we would be perfect and could also control ourselves in every other way.

James 3:2 nlt

You were once darkness, but now you are light in the Lord. Live as children of light.

Ephesians 5:8 niv

Prepare your minds for action, keep sober in spirit, fix your hope completely on the grace to be brought to you at the revelation of Jesus Christ.

1 Peter 1:13 nasb

Serving

You have been called to live in freedom, my brothers and sisters. But don't use your freedom to satisfy your sinful nature. Instead, use your freedom to serve one another in love.

GALATIANS 5:13 NLT

"The more lowly your service to others, the greater you are. To be the greatest, be a servant. But those who think themselves great shall be disappointed and humbled; and those who humble themselves shall be exalted."

MATTHEW 23:11–12 TLB

"Even the Son of Man did not come to be served, but to serve, and to give His life a ransom for many."

MARK 10:45 NASB

"He who is greatest among you, let him be as the younger, and he who governs as he who serves. For who is greater, he who sits at the table, or he who serves? Is it not he who sits at the table? Yet I am among you as the One who serves."

LUKE 22:26–27 NKJV

Stress

The Lord also will be a refuge...in times of trouble.
Those who know Your name will put their trust in You;
For You, Lord, have not forsaken those who seek You.

PSALM 9:9–10 NKJV

"So don't be anxious about tomorrow. God will take care of your tomorrow too. Live one day at a time."

MATTHEW 6:34 TLB

Commit your actions to the Lord,
and your plans will succeed.

PROVERBS 16:3 NLT

"Blessed is the one who trusts in the Lord,
whose confidence is in him.
They will be like a tree planted by the water
that sends out its roots by the stream.
It does not fear when heat comes;
its leaves are always green.
It has no worries in a year of drought
and never fails to bear fruit."

JEREMIAH 17:7–8 NIV

May the God who gives endurance and encouragement give you the same attitude of mind toward each other that Christ Jesus had.

ROMANS 15:5 NIV

Support

Whom have I in heaven but you?
And earth has nothing I desire besides you.
My flesh and my heart may fail,
but God is the strength of my heart
and my portion forever.

PSALM 73:25–26 NIV

The everlasting God is your place of safety,
and his arms will hold you up forever.

DEUTERONOMY 33:27 NCV

God will never forget the needy;
the hope of the afflicted will never perish.

PSALM 9:18 NIV

You are my hiding place;
You shall preserve me from trouble;
You shall surround me with songs of deliverance.

PSALM 32:7 NKJV

"Behold, I am with you always, to the end of the age."

MATTHEW 28:20 ESV

Our steps are made firm by the LORD,
when he delights in our way;
though we stumble, we shall not fall headlong,
for the LORD holds us by the hand.

PSALM 37:23–24 NRSV

Teaching

All scripture is inspired by God and is useful for teaching, for reproof, for correction, and for training in righteousness, so that everyone who belongs to God may be proficient, equipped for every good work.

2 Timothy 3:16-17 nrsv

Let each generation tell its children of your mighty acts; let them proclaim your power.

Psalm 145:4 nlt

I will open my mouth in a parable;
I will utter dark sayings from of old,
things that we have heard and known,
that our ancestors have told us.
We will not hide them from their children;
we will tell to the coming generation
the glorious deeds of the Lord, and his might,
and the wonders that he has done.

Psalm 78:2-4 nrsv

"Go therefore and make disciples of all the nations, baptizing them in the name of the Father and of the Son and of the Holy Spirit, teaching them to observe all things that I have commanded you."

Matthew 28:19-20 nkjv

No discipline seems pleasant at the time, but painful. Later on, however, it produces a harvest of righteousness and peace for those who have been trained by it.

Hebrews 12:11 niv

Thankfulness

Rejoice always, pray without ceasing, in everything give thanks; for this is the will of God.

1 THESSALONIANS 5:16–18 NKJV

Enter his gates with thanksgiving,
and his courts with praise!
Give thanks to him; bless his name!
For the LORD is good;
his steadfast love endures forever,
and his faithfulness to all generations.

PSALM 100:4–5 ESV

Let us come into his presence with thanksgiving;
let us make a joyful noise to him with songs of praise!

PSALM 95:2 ESV

Let us continually offer up a sacrifice of praise to God, that is, the fruit of lips that give thanks to His name.

HEBREWS 13:15 NASB

We give thanks to God always for you, making mention of you in our prayers; constantly bearing in mind your work of faith and labor of love and steadfastness of hope.

1 THESSALONIANS 1:2–3 NASB

Give thanks to the LORD, for he is good;
his love endures forever.

1 CHRONICLES 16:34 NIV

Trust

God, the source of hope, will fill you completely with joy and peace because you trust in him. Then you will overflow with confident hope through the power of the Holy Spirit.

ROMANS 15:13 NLT

The LORD is my strength and my shield;
my heart trusts in him, and he helps me.

PSALM 28:7 NIV

May your whole self—spirit, soul, and body—be kept safe and without fault when our Lord Jesus Christ comes. You can trust the One who calls you to do that for you.

1 THESSALONIANS 5:23–24 NCV

God's way is perfect.
All the LORD's promises prove true.
He is a shield for all who look to him for protection.
For who is God except the LORD?
Who but our God is a solid rock?

PSALM 18:30–31 NLT

Those who know Your name will put their trust in You;
For You, LORD, have not forsaken those who seek You.

PSALM 9:10 NKJV

My God shall supply all your needs according to His riches in glory by Christ Jesus.

PHILIPPIANS 4:19 NKJV

Truth

The very essence of your words is truth;
all your just regulations will stand forever.

PSALM 119:160 NLT

"If you hold to my teaching, you are really my disciples.
Then you will know the truth, and the truth will set you free."

JOHN 8:31–32 NIV

Teach me your ways, O LORD,
that I may live according to your truth!
Grant me purity of heart,
so that I may honor you.

PSALM 86:11 NLT

"When he, the Spirit of truth, comes, he will guide you into
all the truth."

JOHN 16:13 NIV

Truthful words stand the test of time,
but lies are soon exposed.

PROVERBS 12:19 NLT

Let us not love with words or speech but with actions and in
truth.

1 JOHN 3:18 NIV

You desire truth in the innermost being,
And in the hidden part You will make me know wisdom.

PSALM 51:6 NASB

Understanding

Blessed is the one who finds wisdom,
and the one who gets understanding.

PROVERBS 3:13 ESV

The unfolding of your words gives light;
it gives understanding to the simple.

PSALM 119:130 NIV

Cry out for wisdom,
and beg for understanding.
Search for it like silver,
and hunt for it like hidden treasure.
Then you will understand respect for the LORD,
and you will find that you know God.

PROVERBS 2:3-5 NCV

What we have received is not the spirit of the world, but the
Spirit who is from God, so that we may understand what God
has freely given us.

1 CORINTHIANS 2:12 NIV

Be filled with the knowledge of His will in all spiritual wisdom
and understanding, so that you will walk in a manner worthy
of the Lord… and increasing in the knowledge of God.

COLOSSIANS 1:9-10 NASB

Do not let wisdom and understanding out of your sight,
preserve sound judgment and discretion;
they will be life for you.

PROVERBS 3:21-22 NIV

Wisdom

Blessed are those who find wisdom,
those who gain understanding,
for she is more profitable than silver
and yields better returns than gold.
She is more precious than rubies;
nothing you desire can compare with her.
Long life is in her right hand;
in her left hand are riches and honor.
Her ways are pleasant ways,
and all her paths are peace.

PROVERBS 3:13–17 NIV

The wisdom from above is first of all pure. It is also peace loving, gentle at all times, and willing to yield to others. It is full of mercy and good deeds. It shows no favoritism and is always sincere.

JAMES 3:17 NLT

Oh, the depth of the riches both of the wisdom and knowledge of God!

ROMANS 11:33 NASB

Do not let wisdom and understanding out of your sight,
preserve sound judgment and discretion;
they will be life for you.

PROVERBS 3:21–22 NIV

If any of you lacks wisdom, you should ask God,
who gives generously to all without finding fault,
and it will be given to you.

JAMES 1:5 NIV

Worry

Don't worry about anything; instead, pray about everything. Tell God what you need, and thank him for all he has done. Then you will experience God's peace, which exceeds anything we can understand. His peace will guard your hearts and minds as you live in Christ Jesus.

PHILIPPIANS 4:6–7 NLT

"Which of you by worrying can add a single hour to his life's span?"

LUKE 12:25 NASB

Worry weighs a person down;
an encouraging word cheers a person up.

PROVERBS 12:25 NLT

"Do not worry about your life, what you will eat or drink; or about your body, what you will wear. Is not life more than food, and the body more than clothes? Look at the birds of the air; they do not sow or reap or store away in barns, and yet your heavenly Father feeds them. Are you not much more valuable than they?"

MATTHEW 6:25–26 NIV

May the Lord of peace himself give you peace
at all times in every way.

2 THESSALONIANS 3:16 ESV

Give your burdens to the LORD,
and he will take care of you.

PSALM 55:22 NLT